Her cheeky sister Poppy catapults onto David's legs and gets to work untying his bootlaces. And . . .

WHUMP!

Pablo arrives! He plonks onto David's lap and wriggles his bony bottom until he's comfortable.

David has spent his whole life getting close to nature, and it all started with . . .

. . . a fire salamander.

It's spectacular!

It was the perfect gift for David's eighth birthday.

Born in 1926, David grew up in Leicester with his two brothers. He was always fascinated by nature. Every day, he'd set off to catch newts . . .

or pedal across the countryside leaving no stone unturned in his quest for fossils.

At night, while tucked up in bed, David's books seemed to come alive with scuttling beetles and howling wolves. And as he closed his eyes, birds of paradise danced through his dreams. He couldn't wait to meet them all in the wild.

But three important letters would arrive before David's adventures could begin. The first came in 1945.

Dear Mr. Attenborough:

On behalf of Cambridge University, I am delighted to offer you a scholarship to study geology and zoology . . .

David hoped science would be his ticket to explore the wild outdoors, but instead it led him from classrooms to laboratories.

When he graduated in 1947, a second letter arrived.
Perhaps this time his adventure could begin?

NATIONAL SERVICES ACT
ENLISTMENT NOTICE
MINISTER OF LABOUR AND
NATIONAL SERVICE REGIONAL OFFICE

DEAR SIR,
In accordance with the
National Services Act,
you are called upon
for service in the
Royal Navy . . .

But David's travels would have to wait for two years while he worked on boats in North Wales and Scotland.

By 1952, David was married and was just starting his family when a third letter changed everything. It was from the BBC and it said . . .

We've got this funny thing going on in north London.

It involves pictures.

When David strode into the BBC Television Studios in 1952, he had no idea what would be waiting for him – after all, he didn't even own a TV! He got straight to work behind the camera, making live shows about everything from knitting to gardening. Then something much more lively came along – animals from London Zoo.

They didn't always behave . . .

That is NOT a toilet!

David thought there had to be a better way to help people experience nature. That's when he had an idea to film animals in their natural habitats. The programme would be called . . .

. . . Zoo Quest!

And so, in 1954, David set off to film some of Earth's strangest and most mysterious creatures.

He was producer,

sierra leone

director,

sound man,

Greetings from Borneo

animal wrangler

and eventually a presenter too.

Yet of all the extraordinary places
David visited, the most magical was . . .

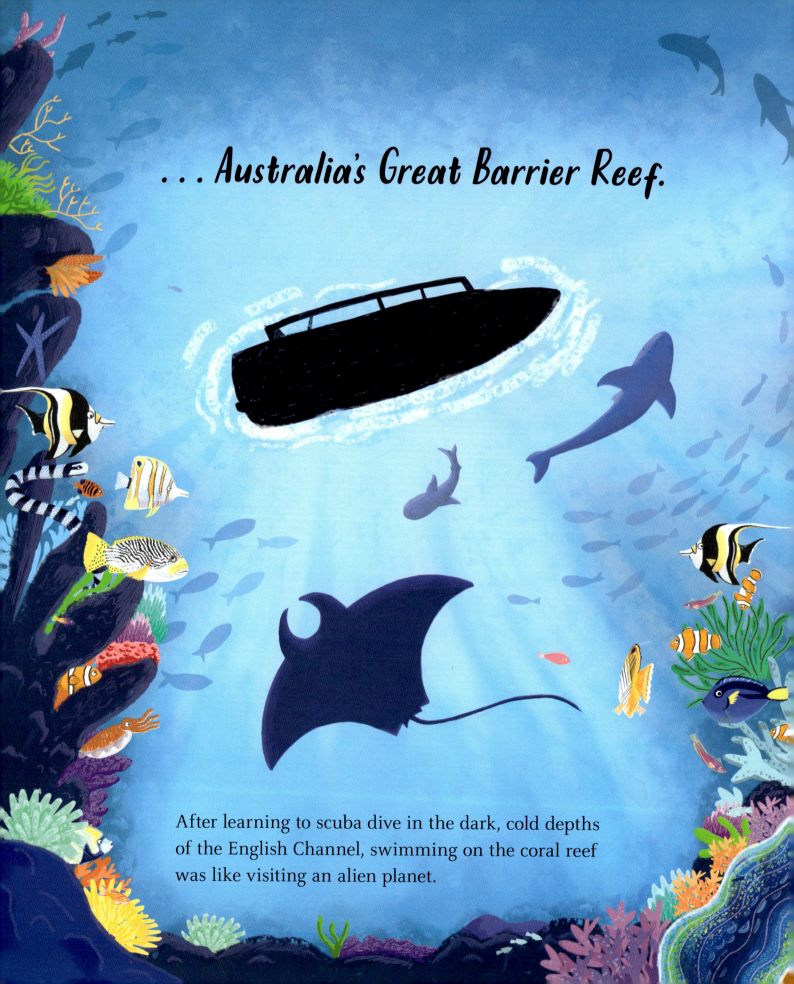

...Australia's Great Barrier Reef.

After learning to scuba dive in the dark, cold depths of the English Channel, swimming on the coral reef was like visiting an alien planet.

The reef shimmered in every colour of the rainbow, bustling with creatures that David had no idea even existed. And with a shake of his flipper, he could float off in any direction he pleased. In that moment, David's lifetime fascination with the reef unfurled.

On every new adventure that followed, David got closer and closer to nature – sometimes too close . . .

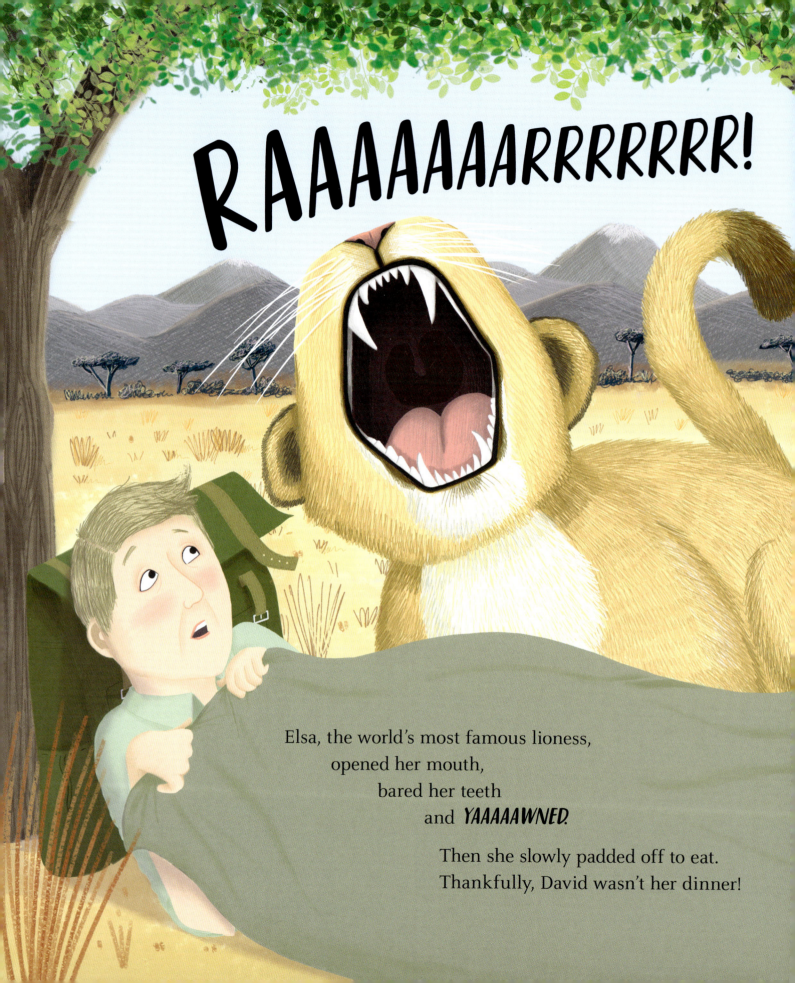

RAAAAAAARRRRRRR!

Elsa, the world's most famous lioness,
opened her mouth,
bared her teeth
and *YAAAAAWNED.*

Then she slowly padded off to eat.
Thankfully, David wasn't her dinner!

Orphaned as a cub, Elsa was raised by humans, then set free to live on Africa's grassy plains. Now in 1960, with cubs of her own, she'd come back to visit her human parents. David had flown out to film the reunion, but when he arrived, Elsa was nowhere to be found. Tired from the long journey, David nodded off, only to wake up to the smelly scent of lion's breath!

When it came to watching David's adventures, viewers felt like they were really there – even though at that time TV programmes were in black and white. But what if David could tell his stories in all their dazzling splendour?

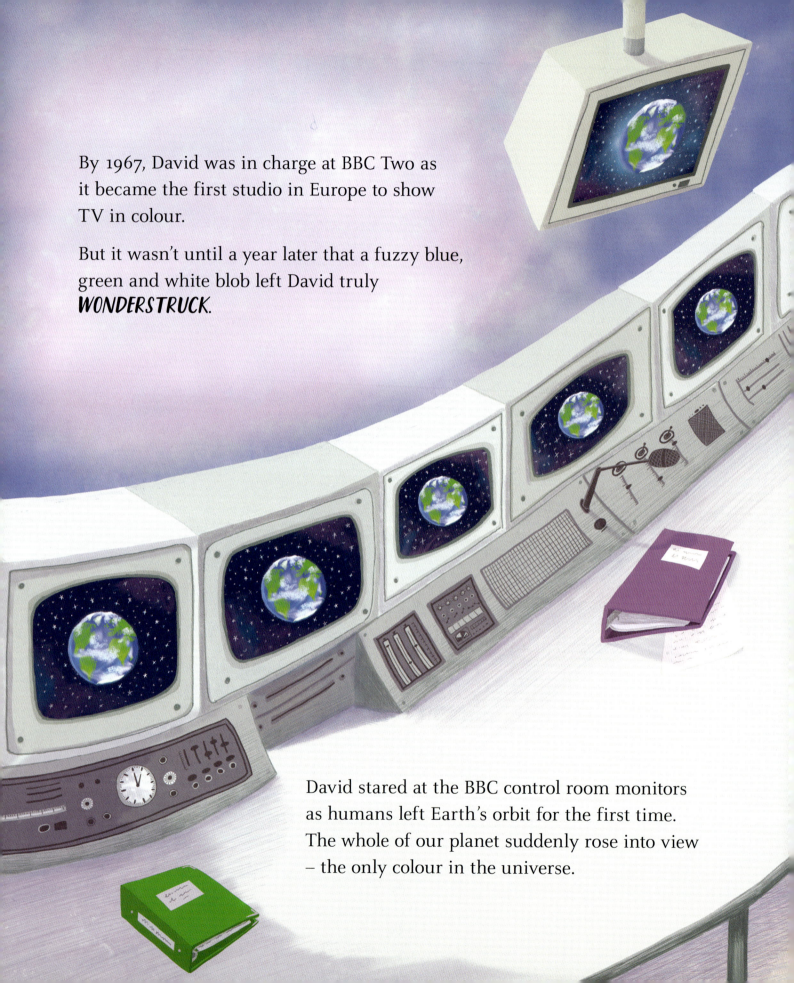

By 1967, David was in charge at BBC Two as it became the first studio in Europe to show TV in colour.

But it wasn't until a year later that a fuzzy blue, green and white blob left David truly **WONDERSTRUCK**.

David stared at the BBC control room monitors as humans left Earth's orbit for the first time. The whole of our planet suddenly rose into view – the only colour in the universe.

The big wide world was calling to David once more, and he couldn't resist heading off on another adventure, this time to tell the story of *Life on Earth*.

In 1979, 500 million people eagerly watched on as David traced the history of all life on our planet.

From fish that clambered onto land 350 million years ago,

and the extinction of dinosaurs

to those scene-stealing gorillas in Rwanda – our closest cousins.

After three years of filming in 30 countries, *Life on Earth* was David's greatest achievement.

And on the dark, damp forest floor of New Guinea's jungle, the bird of paradise amazed viewers as it struck a pose. It puffed out its feathers like an umbrella and frantically danced about, bobbing and bouncing, as its beady blue eyes bulged.

It was one of more than 600 species of plants and animals whose stories David shared with the world.

He had become a **VOICE FOR NATURE.**

David had already travelled millions of kilometres across the planet. And with the help of new technology, he found he could go

FURTHER,

HIGHER

and **DEEPER** than he had ever gone before.

Still, each new adventure had its obstacles. When David visited Christmas Island in the Indian Ocean, there were 50 million of them!

As the wet season's first raindrops fell, Christmas Island's red crabs scuttled from their forest burrows to drop their eggs in the ocean. Just before dawn, a wave of crabs surged towards the sea. They clambered up and over everything in their path – including David!

OUCH!

By the time David was in his nineties, he had visited every continent on Earth, meeting all sorts of creatures from the extraordinary to the rare . . .

I thought you were extinct!

On the Galápagos Islands in the Pacific Ocean, David lay on his belly and waited for Lonesome George, a Pinta Island tortoise, to open his eyes. Eventually, George stuck out his head and yawned. His hundred-year-old body creaked as he slowly ambled away.

Thousands of giant tortoises once lived across the Galápagos Islands, but when humans arrived on ships in the seventeenth century, they left with the tortoises as food. One by one, the Pinta Island tortoises disappeared. George surprised everyone when he trudged out of the bushes in 1971. Scientists hoped they'd find another Pinta Island tortoise to keep him company, but they never did.

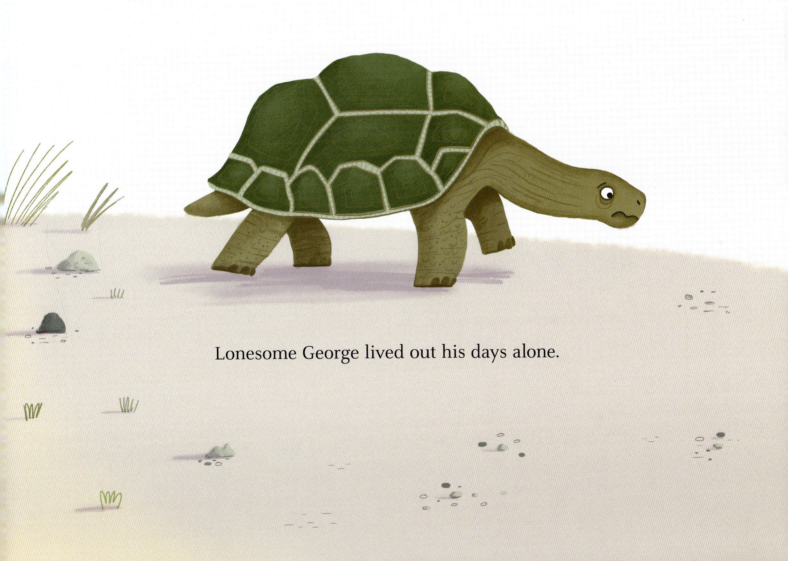

Lonesome George lived out his days alone.

As the years passed, David met too many animals who had lost their homes and lives because of changes happening to our planet.

Everywhere he went, he found rainforests were being cut down,

the ice was melting,

and the ocean bobbed with plastic.

David had seen too much not to say something.

So as he headed back out on his travels, instead of meeting animals, he met princes, presidents and protestors.

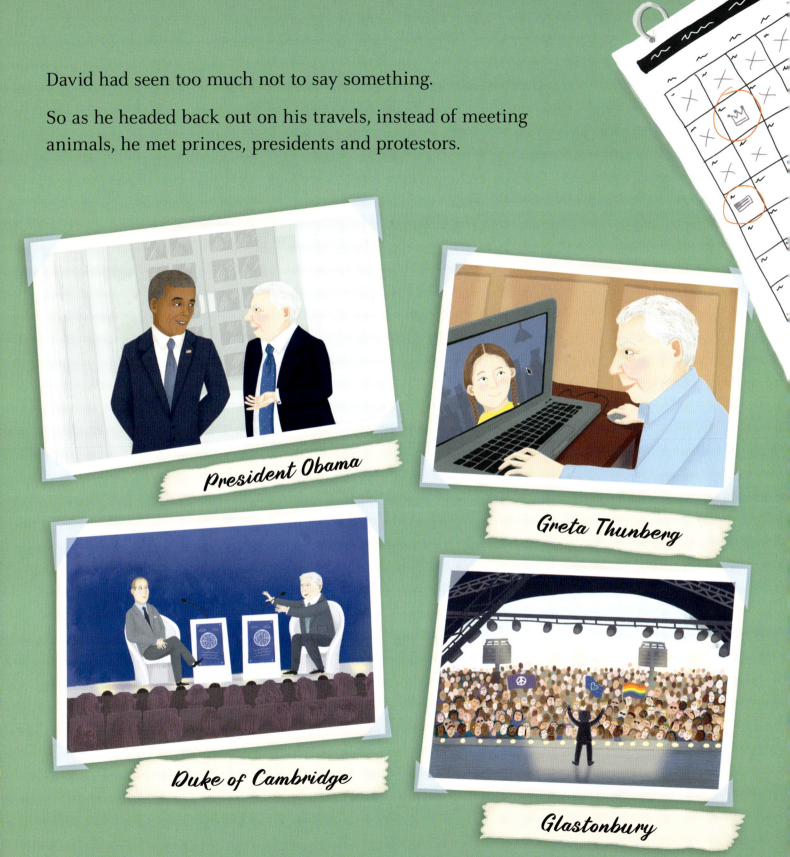

President Obama

Greta Thunberg

Duke of Cambridge

Glastonbury

He had become a **FORCE OF NATURE**, calling for Earth's protection.

Now, after almost 70 years on TV, making hundreds of TV shows and travelling far enough to reach the Moon, David still thinks there's no place like home.

Even so, every so often, David pulls on his
favourite blue shirt and heads off on another
extraordinary adventure in his

WILD LIFE!

Meet the animals from David's adventures!

Lionesses do most of the hunting for the pride, working together to catch speedy prey.

Giant tortoises can survive for up to a year without food or water.

Mountain gorillas are some of our closest animal relatives.

Sloths do everything slowly – they can take up to a month to digest a single leaf!

The male bird of paradise makes a dancefloor, then *clears* the dancefloor with its fancy moves as it woos the female.

Fire salamanders smell like vanilla. Their black and yellow colouring means "watch out, I'm poisonous!"

David kept the fire salamander tradition by giving one to his son Robert on his eighth birthday.

Komodo dragons are the largest species of lizard on the planet, weighing as much as a human adult!

Christmas Island red crabs are land crabs. They can't swim!

Armadillos are the only mammals to have a shell.

Welcome to the Museum!

By the time David was seven, he'd made his own mini-museum to house the treasures he found on his adventures such as grass-snake skins and bird eggs. An archaeologist friend of his father's was so impressed by David's collection that she sent him a box of dried seahorses and other fossils to add to it. Her curiosities helped inspire David to become a naturalist, just as David has inspired generations of scientists and conservationists too. Many have even named their discoveries after him. So in a way, David's mini-museum continues to grow!

Prethopalpus attenboroughi
A 1-mm-long goblin spider, Australia.

Microleo attenboroughi
An extinct kitten-sized
marsupial lion, Australia.

Pristimantis attenboroughi
A tree frog, Peru.

Electrotettix attenboroughi
A 20-million-year-old grasshopper
found in amber, Dominican Republic.

Mesosticta davidattenboroughi
A 100-million-year-old damselfly
found in amber, Myanmar.

Zaglossus attenboroughi
A long-beaked echidna, last seen
in the 1960s, New Guinea.

Attenborougharion rubicundus
A colourful forest snail,
Australia.

Nepenthes attenboroughii
A rodent-digesting pitcher
plant, Philippines.

Platysaurus attenboroughi
A flat lizard, South Africa
and Namibia.

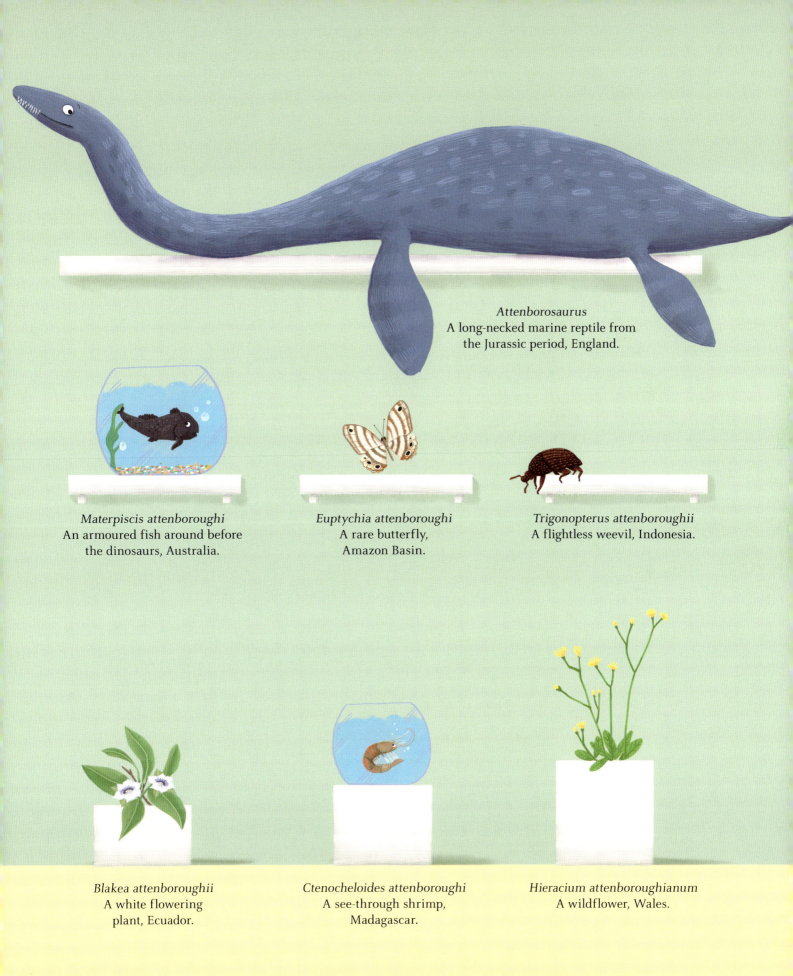

Attenborosaurus
A long-necked marine reptile from
the Jurassic period, England.

Materpiscis attenboroughi
An armoured fish around before
the dinosaurs, Australia.

Euptychia attenboroughi
A rare butterfly,
Amazon Basin.

Trigonopterus attenboroughii
A flightless weevil, Indonesia.

Blakea attenboroughii
A white flowering
plant, Ecuador.

Ctenocheloides attenboroughi
A see-through shrimp,
Madagascar.

Hieracium attenboroughianum
A wildflower, Wales.

For Sir David, whose stories inspire
all of mine – L.S.S.

For Dean, with love – H.S. x

First published in Great Britain in 2022 by Wren & Rook

HB ISBN: 978 1 5263 6415 9
PB ISBN: 978 1 5263 6417 3
E-book ISBN: 978 1 5263 6416 6
10 9 8 7 6 5 4 3 2 1

Wren & Rook
An imprint of
Hachette Children's Group
Part of Hodder & Stoughton
Carmelite House
50 Victoria Embankment
London EC4Y 0DZ

An Hachette UK Company
www.hachette.co.uk
www.hachettechildrens.co.uk

Printed in China